PARTY PAPER
Making Clever Invitations & Decorations

Christian Sanladerer

Sterling Publishing Co., Inc.   New York

Library of Congress Cataloging-in-Publication Data

Sanladerer, Christian.
    [Schmuck- und Glückwunschkarten. English]
    Party paper : making clever invitations & decorations / Christian Sanladerer.
        p.   cm.
    Translation of: Schmuck- und Glückwunschkarten.
    Includes index.
    ISBN 0-8069-8458-9
    1. Greeting cards.   2. Paper work.   I. Title.
TT872.S2613   1991
745.594′ 1–dc20   91-15228
                                                       CIP

10 9 8 7 6 5 4 3 2 1

First paperback edition published in 1992 by
Sterling Publishing Company, Inc.
387 Park Avenue South, New York, N.Y. 10016
English translation © 1991 by Sterling Publishing Company
Original edition published in Germany under the title
Schmuck- und Glückwunschkarten © 1990 by
Falken-Verlag GmbH, Niedemhausen/Ts.
Distributed in Canada by Sterling Publishing
℅ Canadian Manda Group, P.O. Box 920, Station U
Toronto, Ontario, Canada M8Z 5P9
Distributed in Great Britain and Europe by Cassell PLC
Villiers House, 41/47 Strand, London WC2N 5JE, England
Distributed in Australia by Capricorn Link Ltd.
P.O. Box 665, Lane Cove, NSW 2066
Printed in China
All rights reserved

Sterling   ISBN 0-8069-8458-9   Trade
           0-8069-8459-7   Paper

CONTENTS

Preface 5
Paper, A Traditional Material 6
  Manufacturing Methods 6
  A Many-Faceted Material 7
Paper & Accessories 8
Collage Cards 11
  Technique 12
  Samples 14
Folding Cards 23
  Technique 24
  Samples 26
Paper Architecture 35
  Technique 36
  Experiment with Color 38
  Tips for Your Own Creations 39
  Samples 40
Envelopes 52
  Samples 52
Patterns 58
Index 96

Translated by Elisabeth R. Reinersmann

English translation edited by Keith L. Schiffman

Preface

This book salutes the wonderful old tradition of bringing joy to loved ones by sending written or illustrated greetings. It's the art of handcrafted greeting cards.

Ever since paper was invented, it's borne messages of appreciation, and symbolic expressions of courteous manners. Originally, the New Year was the most important occasion for sending greeting cards. People soon found many more reasons for sending personal signs of appreciation and congratulations.

After the development of the woodcut and copperplate engraving methods in the 15th century, it became feasible to make duplicates from an original design or print. The popularity of greeting cards then increased greatly. The exchange of written and illustrated greeting cards as a sign of affection reached a high point in the 18th and 19th centuries, when these cards became *extremely* fashionable.

With the increased improvement of manual printing techniques and the onset of industrialization, small greeting cards slowly replaced the large-format cards that often consisted of several pages.

A wide array of lovingly designed paper creations appeared—folded letters and cards with three-dimensional pop-up designs—every one of them more than just practical. Due to advances made in the methods of production, these artfully created, elaborate greeting cards were eventually replaced by the mass-produced (and rather primitive) picture postcard.

Although there's an endless selection of greeting cards available to suit almost any conceivable occasion, sometimes we just can't find an appropriate card for a specific occasion or for that special person. Inevitably, we start thinking of making our

own. The card would then fit the taste and the interest of a particular person, or of a specific occasion—a card made to order! As gifts and gift wrapping become increasingly personalized, the greeting card has also become a way of showing how much thought was given to the gift's recipient.

This book introduces the art of creating cards made from paper and/or construction paper. These materials are almost as easy to work with as they are to obtain. I've purposely chosen designs that differ from the ones you'd find in a card shop. Included here are designs for all those important festive occasions: birthdays, Christmas, Easter, engagements, and weddings. I've also included some designs for cards without any particular theme.

These cards can be sent throughout the year, and they can also be displayed, adding a special decorative touch to any room. Although I only discuss three techniques, these techniques will, nevertheless, apply to countless motifs of varying levels of difficulty, and they will also serve as a survey of the many greeting-card creations in existence. Precise instructions at the beginning of each chapter and patterns for every card will allow you to duplicate each item without any difficulty. In addition, I've included a chapter showing you how to make your own envelopes. These envelopes will free you from dependence upon standard, store-bought envelopes and they'll allow you to give *everything* your personal touch.

Each of the examples included in this book demonstrates how to create (with inexpensive materials and with a little manual dexterity) the most charming cards. With a bit of imagination and skill, the possibilities are limitless.

PAPER, A TRADITIONAL MATERIAL

Ever since man desired to record his experiences and to maintain those records for posterity, he's searched for the perfect way to capture these experiences—in pictures, symbols, or in writing. Nature provided him with quite a selection of materials to record his actions: stone, clay, wood, animal skins, and wax. Each medium had its disadvantages: Some were too heavy, some were too cumbersome, some weren't stable enough. The search for a better medium continued.

First came the Sumerian cuneiform clay tablets. Much later, the Egyptians developed papyrus. This material, made from the papyrus plant, gives paper its name. Until the 10th century A.D., papyrus was the most commonly used communication medium in the Western world. The disadvantage of papyrus was that its fragile structure did not tolerate folding; one had to glue individual pieces together and roll them up for storage. The search for a more flexible and stable material resulted in the development of parchment (the material and the name came from Pergamon, in Asia Minor). Parchment was made from animal skins from which the hair had been removed. Until the general introduction of paper, parchment was used in Europe to make books. Folding, binding, and storage were never problems with parchment.

From the 12th century B.C., bamboo tablets and small wooden tablets were used in Asia to record and convey messages. About 300 B.C. people first began experimenting with lightweight silk. Much like Egyptian papyrus, sheets of written and illustrated silk were joined into volumes and rolls of varying sizes and lengths.

Perhaps because silk was so expensive, attempts were soon made to use silk leftovers (threads and fibres) to produce a writing surface. Silk, as opposed to material made from plant sources, was made from fibres produced by the silkworm. Silk had no sticky qualities, and all attempts to produce a writing surface ended in failure.

Towards the end of the first century A.D., Ts'ai Lun of China successfully produced a material good enough to write upon. He used tree bark, leftovers from the production of hemp rope, discarded fishnets and rags. To him is accorded the distinction of having invented paper.

Manufacturing Methods

To produce this type of writing surface, the basic material is first ground up using a big stone mortar and pestle, and then mixed with water in large tubs. This produces a material with a mushy consistency. To make sheets of paper from this mush, the water must be extracted by using large strainers specially made from grass and bamboo. Shaking the strainers distributes the fibres evenly and allows the water to drain off.

Organic substances then mat together and, after a sufficient drying time and a smoothing and cleaning process, the result is a very effective writing surface. This manual process was the beginning of the paper industry. It took many centuries for the news about this sensational papermaking method to reach the rest of the world. After many centuries, in Japan, papermaking became an independent and highly respected art form.

It was not until the 8th century A.D. that the knowledge of paper finally reached the West. When the Chinese lost a battle at Samarkand, Chinese prisoners were forced (under the threat of death) to divulge the secret of papermaking to the victors.

Samarkand then became the main producer and supplier of paper in the Islamic world, which stretched to Morocco and southern Spain.

This new material served as the base for a highly developed writing art. Islamic accomplishments in science and literature grew at an unprecedented rate. In the 12th century, paper was produced for the first time in Morocco and in southern Spain and was exported from there to Europe in the beginning of the 13th century. Italy, before any other part of Europe, began producing its own paper, thereby freeing itself from dependence upon the Arabs. Other regions followed, but it took nearly 400 years before paper was routinely produced all across Europe. From Europe, paper made its way to the Americas and, eventually, paper was produced worldwide.

More than anything else, the rapid spread of printing in Europe in the 15th century was responsible for the equally rapid spread of paper production. New demands were made on paper: Manual papermaking took too long, and with high demand, paper became very expensive. The beginning of industrialization in the 18th century also brought with it industrial paper production.

Today paper is mass-produced. While the basic methods of production are the same as they were hundreds of years ago, the tools and the materials have improved. Papermaking today is a highly complex, computer-controlled process. The details of this process go beyond the scope of this book. However, let's mention some of the material used in the process. Modern paper (depending upon its intended use) contains rag fibres, wood pulp and cellulose. Some paper fibres also come from specific types of grass, such as wheat and rye grasses. In recent times fillers have been added, like plaster, kaolin, and other substances extracted from the soil. These substances fill in the gaps between the organic fibres, giving paper its smooth surface. Adding lime gives paper its stability and actually makes writing on paper possible. The varied shades of paper are the result of a dyeing process. The result of all this technology is the ability to produce a wide range of paper with many different qualities, satisfying a wide range of needs.

A Many-Faceted Material

Paper, being such an integral part of our lives, is generally taken for granted. Paper constantly provides us with information in the form of printed texts and pictures—like the pages of this book. Paper provides packaging material (usually discarded as soon as it's removed), or it makes napkins, coffee filtres, or streamers. But we would not be doing justice to this unique material if we saw it only from a practical point of view.

Paper is also an intriguing substance, useful as an adjunct to the creative process. This aspect has long been neglected in Europe, while in Asia the creative utilization of paper has been a prominent tradition for centuries (origami comes immediately to mind). This should not come as a surprise, since Asia is the original source of paper.

Working with paper demands concentration and patience. Asians, influenced to a great degree by their practice of meditation, seem to be particularly adept at crafts that demand these traits. Paper is an ideal medium for the expression of the Asians' aesthetic sense and for their ability to reduce concepts and matter to their essentials.

It is no coincidence that in Asia paper has long been an intricate part of daily life. Some of the well-known paper products of the Far East are lanterns, umbrellas, fans, masks, and a wide variety of toys. Even in traditional Asian architecture, paper plays a significant role—in Japan wall coverings and sliding doors are made from rice paper.

During the Art Nouveau period, when European interest in Asian culture grew, many Chinese and Japanese paper articles made their way to Europe. However, paper never reached the degree of importance in Europe that it held in the Far East.

Today, however, paper is experiencing a real boom. With the rediscovery of old techniques and traditions, people are again taking a good look at paper and all the fascinating possibilities it provides for creative expression.

This book explores one of these intriguing areas: creating notepaper and greeting cards.

PAPER & ACCESSORIES

Paper is fascinating because of its contradictory qualities: It's pliable, but it's also very strong. Paper's character allows it to be used in many different ways: It can be folded and creased, torn, cut, and glued. Paper: Punch holes in it, print on it . . . One more advantage: Paper's light weight makes it manageable even when it's used for large projects.

If you want good results when you create paper projects, don't skimp on materials. Have an assortment of paper of different strengths and colors close at hand. You'll have more to choose from, and you won't restrict your creativity by not having the right color or the right type of paper at hand. How annoying it would be not to be able to spontaneously turn an idea into reality because the right color was missing. Making your own cards makes buying a great assortment of paper a really good investment. The paper industry is making available an unbelievably rich assortment of paper of many different qualities, for utilitarian as well as for decorative purposes.

Typing paper is available in almost every household and is very useful for sketching and for testing folds and creases. The process of converting ideas into folding cards can be tested inexpensively using this paper.

High-quality sketch pads have paper that is free of wood pulp. The paper is thus insensitive to light, and it won't yellow. This stiff, smooth paper is best for greeting cards. Pencil marks can be easily erased from this paper. It can be folded cleanly, and a bigger-than-normal card won't collapse.

One type of sketch-pad paper that's somewhat rougher does not lend itself well to folding purposes, because its edges tend to fray easily and pencil marks are difficult to remove.

Construction paper is very inexpensive and comes in many different colors. The paper is dyed during the pulp stage, and both sides can be used. It is, however, rather porous and only a very limited amount of glue should be used. Once applied, glue leaves telltale stains.

Construction paper is sensitive to light, and colors bleach out easily, sometimes only after a very short time. This paper is best suited for temporary projects, where stable colors are not important.

Bristol board (in many surface finishes) is somewhat stiffer than construction paper. It's ideal when used as a base for collages, folding cards or pop-up cards.

High-gloss paper, originally intended for children's use, has a glossy finish and comes in a few, strong colors on one side only. The finish ensures that the colors won't fade.

High-quality colored paper (Pantone®) is a paper primarily used in the graphics and design industries. Its colors are highly stable, applied to one side only, and are available in nearly every color imaginable—you'll be able to create almost any color combination you can think of.

The paper comes in high-gloss and mat finishes and it's somewhat more expensive than either construction paper or high-gloss paper. Use this paper when you want to impress somebody, or when you build projects of a more permanent character.

Grain indicates the direction of the flow of the paper as it moves over the strainer and the drums. The fibres in the pulp arrange themselves during this process parallel to the direction of the movement of the strainer and the drums. (Paper's grain runs lengthwise.)

When making the initial, main fold, make sure that the fold runs across the grain (at a right angle to the grain). Folding this way assures greater stability of your project, particularly if it's a pop-up design. If a fold runs parallel to the grain, it has a tendency to buckle and weaken the sheet of paper and the structure.

The direction of the grain can easily be determined. Make a fold. If the folding is easy and you feel no resistance, the fold runs parallel to the grain. If you feel a definite resistance, the fold runs at a right angle to the grain.

The choice of proper tools is as important as choosing the right paper. The more improvising you have to do, the less fun you'll have. The following is a list of tools that I think are necessary to achieve the best possible results.

Pencils for drawing cutting lines and folding lines. Use a soft (#2) pencil.

Eraser

Tracing paper for copying patterns.

Protractor

Metal ruler as a guide for cutting and creasing.

Template for drawing small, exact circles.

Compass for drawing large circles.

Hole puncher to make round pieces of paper.

Tweezers to hold very small pieces when gluing, or when making small folds.

Scissors, medium size, but well sharpened.

Utility knife, preferably one with disposable blades, where a used blade can be pushed out and broken off.

Art knife for cutting fine details.

Burnishing tool: a flat, pointed tool with rounded edges, made from bone or synthetic material. Used for reinforcing folds and for applying small amounts of glue to paper.

Cutting board for temporary use. Made from heavy, smooth cardboard (which needs to be changed occasionally) or a permanent base made from synthetic material.

Drawing table makes life much easier when drawing or cutting parallel lines or right-angle lines. A table isn't essential, however, unless you intend to do extensive work.

White glue

Rubber cement for gluing paper temporarily to the base of the card. Rubber cement can be easily removed at any time. Dried-on cement can simply be rubbed off.

Now that you have the basic information and the necessary tools, nothing stands in your way. Ready, set, go!

COLLAGE CARDS

Early in this century collage was introduced by noted artists. The appearance of collage coincided with the appearance of modern art. Even today, collage is an often applied and highly valued technique for creative expression. The name is French (*coller* means to glue) and the name indicates the nature of the process. Many different parts of different colors and shapes, glued to a surface or base, create a unified whole. For our purposes, we'll create a greeting-card design.

What holds true for a work of art, of course, can also be applied here. Greeting cards can be created from many different materials—gift-wrapping paper, pictures from calendars, magazines or newspapers, construction paper in complementary colors, etc.

The examples that follow, however, were purposely limited to smooth, solid-colored paper. I didn't want to expand the scope of this book, but I did want to show the wealth of possibilities this technique has to offer, even with a limited range of material. I wanted to ensure that the paper I recommended was easily available, so that you could easily copy any one of the examples.

11

Illus. 1

Illus. 3

Technique

Choose a theme and start by first making the basic card. The card could either be the same size as the pattern, or you could double the size to make a folding card.

Each pattern is 83% of full size. Use a photocopier at 121% enlargement to get the pattern to full size. This is a standard enlargement on most photocopiers.

Depending upon the way the card is opened (either from the lower edge upwards, or from the right to the left), double either the horizontal or the vertical measurement.

If you want the design to be framed, either in white or in some other color, allow for the extra space that this requires. Be sure that you use the protractor to assure clean right angles, accurate measurements, and balanced frame proportions (see Illus. 1).

Folding cards are folded in the middle. Crease the card in the middle, using the metal ruler as a guide for accuracy (see Illus. 2).

Fold the card in half and reinforce the fold with a burnishing tool, as shown in Illus. 3. You could use your thumbnail—it serves the same purpose. Put the card aside for a moment.

Illus. 2

Illus. 4

Now copy the design you've chosen, as well as its parts, using tracing paper and a #2 pencil. Secure the tracing paper with small pieces of tape (see Illus. 4).

Before you begin to transfer the individual pieces onto the paper in their respective colors and begin to cut, make one master copy of the whole, and pay attention to the following points. When assembling the design, start with the basic surface. In this example the basic surface is the pink background to which all the other parts are attached. A certain amount of overlapping and intersecting of the individual parts is inevitable. Take this into account when tracing the parts (see Illus. 5). Fill in the

missing lines or delete those that are unnecessary. For instance, the little package on the bottom of the cat should logically be one green square, rather than four little ones. The red bow is glued over the whole square afterwards.

So that you don't lose track of things, number the individual parts in the order that they're to be attached (see Illus. 6). You can use this master tracing as a guide to check your progress when you begin to glue. Use a ruler for all straight lines and use the protractor for right angles. Use the compass and/or the template to trace circles and round shapes.

To start, cut out the individual parts

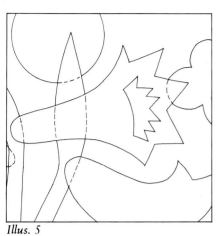

Illus. 5

Illus. 7

Illus. 6

Illus. 8

roughly and sort them according to where they belong (see Illus. 7). Attach them temporarily with a little rubber cement; it can be rubbed off later.

If you're working with one-sided colored paper, do this temporary gluing on the reverse (white) side. Now finish cutting out every piece, exactly aligning the contours and (for now) put them aside with the master (numbered) tracing. For straight cuts use the utility knife, for rounded lines use scissors, and for small shapes use the art knife.

Before you begin gluing, assemble your design and check to see if you have all the necessary parts, that they are all cut properly, and that they fit as intended. If every-thing is in order, begin gluing. Begin with those parts that are closest to the background. First glue the pink background, followed by the black body of the cat, then the white circles for the eyes, and so forth.

Those parts that are closest to the surface, of course, are glued last (see Illus. 8). Glue the blue of the iris, the red ribbon on the package, and the pink whiskers. Start with the largest part; then add the details as if you were covering a bare surface: A house gets its windows and doors, a gift package gets its ribbons and bows.

While you trace a design, make a mental picture of the sequence in which it has to be completed.

When the design is assembled, cover the finished product with a clean sheet of paper and press down on the individual pieces with the ball of your thumb. Now glue the finished design to the card.

A few tips may be helpful for the projects that follow. It's much easier to cut small triangles, squares, or rectangles if the paper you're using is only slightly larger than the shape itself, rather than using a big sheet of paper. Very small circles can be made with a hole puncher. They'll all be the same size, of course.

When you outline or frame something in a different color, first choose the paper you want to use. Make the contrasting background slightly larger, following the shape of the form that you want to outline or frame.

Armed with all these important instructions, you'll have no problems duplicating any of the examples included, or even designing and assembling your own creations.

13

"Love and marriage . . ." The occasion really doesn't matter. A loving message for that special person in your life, an invitation to an informal get-together (at that quiet piano bar?), congratulations for an engagement or a wedding—a card you've made yourself is always appreciated.

The examples speak for themselves.

They're playing our song! Two hearts float on the air. The light blue horizontal stripes on a darker blue give shape and structure to an otherwise blank sky. Two small triangles on each heart give a rounded effect.

A fender bender with a happy ending! Fate may have been smiling on that chance encounter.

A toast! There's always a good reason for opening a bottle of champagne.

Hearts again, each a different size. The dark background, positioned slightly off-center adds dynamism to an already vibrant pattern.

14

Invitation to a trip or greetings from a vacation—these designs are useful for many different occasions.

"Ciao"—saying goodbye before your trip? The letters (on a square background) are stacked like a child's alphabet blocks. Maybe this card will get you a going-away party.

Anyone who gets this "beachy" card (perhaps as a weekend invitation to that beach house) won't hestitate about accepting. Of course, this design will also be appreciated when sent from that exotic vacation to those who had to stay behind.

The party invitation leaves no doubt that there's fun in the making.

How about coming over for coffee and cake? Small pieces of paper have been carefully glued to the cake. The "steam" rising from the coffee cup is paper cut using pinking shears.

A mysterious atmosphere is conjured up by this card and is achieved by the unique color combination. What a costume party this will be! This card is perfect for an invitation to Mardi Gras in New Orleans!

Artfully created greeting cards with different themes are always welcome, especially to celebrate the joy of spring and Easter.

The card below shows off an array of decorated Easter eggs. The card itself is egg-shaped, and it has a frame in a contrasting color that acts as a highlight.

Decorative elements were purposely kept to a minimum on the card depicting a bounding rabbit.

The black background allows the colors to shine particularly bright on the "hen" card. The clear graphic depiction (combined with the balanced shape and posture of the hen) is cheerful, yet dignified.

Cards with a flower motif are always welcome, no matter what the occasion. Stylized lilies on a red background, irregularly outlined in contrasting colors, are purposely angled.

The card (far right) shows blossoms in red, blue, and white, surrounded by soft green-yellow colors. The yellow stamens are arranged in pairs.

Christmas is just around the corner. Sending beautiful cards is a time-honored tradition. The contrast between inside/ outside and warm/cold is perfectly captured by the contrasting colors of the "cat" card on the far left. The shape of the snow under the window is actually "negative space," created by the way the blue of the basic surface was cut. The snowflakes, by the way, will appear more lively when they're cut out by hand. If that seems to be too much trouble, a hole puncher will do the job well.

The Christmas tree is made of simple geometric forms that have been symmetrically arranged. Small triangles (glued to the upper left portion of the Christmas bulbs) are light reflections. They give shape and brilliance to the bulbs.

The little green Christmas trees silhouetted against the night sky add that magical touch to the cityscape.

The examples below are suggestions for New Year's cards. They could, of course, also be sent on other occasions.

If you need some luck, this little pig with the four-leaf clover will bring it to you—at the start of the New Year, before an impending exam, as best wishes for a speedy recovery—you name it!

The mystery of the deep woods is captured on the mushroom card. An interesting design element utilizes white dots for the cap and for the snowflakes.

Challenging the superstition that a black cat means bad luck, this little creature, bearing a gift, also brings you his sincerest best wishes.

21

FOLDING CARDS

In the last chapter we saw how the interplay between color and shape can give depth and character to two-dimensional collage cards. Now let's look at cards whose special charm comes from repeating the card's basic shape one or even several times. This method is two-dimensional, and it also creates a certain spatial effect.

Folding cards are made in much the same way that we once made Christmas stars, with a multiple-folding technique. A square or round sheet of paper was first folded in half, then into quarters, then into eighths, and so on.

Folding cards can be made with either one fold through the middle (as if you were making a collage card), or by folding a piece of paper in several parallel folds (often called accordion folds).

To make accordion folds, first fold a piece of paper in equal, parallel folds, first forward, the next fold backwards, and so on. Cards could retain their rectangular shape, with only a few simple decorations, or they could assume a totally new shape by cutting away the outer edges of the chosen design.

Technique

In order to duplicate any one of the examples shown on the following pages, first cut a rectangular sheet of paper to the required dimensions. The width of the sheet will depend upon the height of the design. The length is determined by how many folds you want to make. Keep in mind the strength of the paper you're using. Remember that cutting difficulty increases with the number of folds.

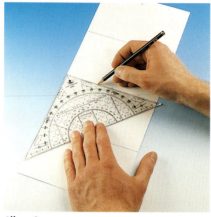
Illus. 9

After you've determined the card's dimensions, draw each folding line (according to your own measurements) with the help of a protractor and a #2 pencil (see Illus. 9). Make sure that every line is at a true right angle. Now (with the tip of the utility knife) score along the lines, using the metal ruler to assure clean folds (see Illus. 10).

Fold the paper accordion-style, the way you want the finished card to look, and use the burnishing tool to reinforce these folds as shown (see Illus. 11). If necessary, use your thumbnail to make the folds crisp.

Illus. 10

Now we'll transfer the pattern to the front of the card. First, tape down the tracing paper over the pattern to prevent the tracing paper from moving. Trace the design of the pattern onto the tracing paper, using a #2 pencil. Remove the tape and turn the tracing paper over. Position the upside-down tracing paper over the face of the card. Burnish the pencil lines (on the other side of the tracing paper) by rubbing over the lines with a soft pencil, as shown in Illus. 12. By following this procedure, you'll transfer your pencil lines to the face of the card.

Secure the tracing paper with a little rubber cement (easily removed afterwards) to prevent it from moving when transferring the design to the face of the card. See the instructions for paper architecture on page 34.

Using a pair of scissors, cut the folded card along the outer edges of the design (see Illus. 13). Use a utility knife and metal ruler to get straight lines.

Illus. 11

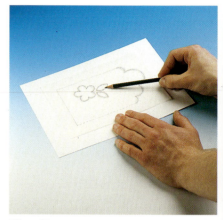
Illus. 12

Illus. 13

Illus. 14

Always make any inside cutouts with the utility knife (see Illus. 14). When working with the utility knife, keep a sturdy pad between your project and the table to protect the tabletop. Because you're cutting through several layers of paper, the utility knife's blades *must* be very sharp.

If you plan to change the design, or if you want to create your own design, be sure that there's enough space between the folded edge of the card and the design. The finished card will have enough stability then. If you cut too much of the folded edge away, the card will fall apart.

Test every new design (typing paper is ideal for testing) before you start on a *real* card. Testing gives you a chance to examine the effect of the design, as well as a sense of the sequence of the steps involved in making the card. Test new ideas before you begin the *real* work.

Some designs for folding cards are so charming that you just might want to leave the cards all white or all one color. You just might want to dispense with *any* added decoration. You might want to decorate only the front page, using various shapes and designs cut from high-gloss paper, as shown in some of the examples on the following pages.

Sometimes interesting effects can be achieved by adding a contrasting color to the back page. Feel free to liven up the inside pages with various accent colors and designs. Highlighting a cutout by gluing paper in contrasting colors to the back of the page is a particularly interesting technique. The following pages show the different effects that can be achieved using these methods.

Here's a tip on gluing contrasting paper to the top page of a folding card. Cut the paper slightly larger than the page to be covered. Remove the excess either with a pair of scissors or with a utility knife, following the edges of the card. This creates a clean edge and ensures that the paper fits the design (see Illus. 15). Add the other

Illus. 15

Illus. 16

parts of the design one at a time, as was discussed in the chapter on collage cards (see Illus. 16).

No matter what you've chosen—a card without any added decoration, or one where you've given free rein to your creativity—it's really very easy to make a folding card using the techniques just described. Don't be afraid to create your own!

These folding cards will delight not only children. The colorful rabbit and the elephant can be made as single cards or as multiple folding cards with rows of identical siblings. Too many layers of paper, however, may mean that you can't cut the outline of the form all at once.

An oversize mouse, sent in an equally oversize envelope, will thrill the lucky recipient.

A row of houses completes this animal scene. This project is a good example of the effects that can be achieved with simple forms and white paper alone. It's all right to dispense with any additional, colorful decoration. This card could be used for a house-warming invitation or as a notification of your new address.

Why not make the *card* the gift? These four examples show four variations on the same theme. In every instance we changed the basic form, the shape of the bow, and the pattern on the paper. Squares, triangles, dots, and stripes have been liberally spread over the front page. On each card, only the front page has been decorated.

If you like, you could carry the theme of the card to the inside (sparingly perhaps, and reduced in shape or size), or you might want to give the back of the card a "happy face."

The Christmas tree reveals its full beauty only after the card has been fully opened. You could decorate only the front page, leaving the back white, or you could carry the theme to the back page and reverse the colors—a red tree with golden bulbs and green stars!

Say it with a card. The themes of these cards fit many occasions.

If you have to decline an invitation, you'll surely be forgiven if you send this "sorry" card. Did you forget your wedding anniversary, by some chance?

At first glance, the thank-you note appears rather plain, but wait until it's opened! The back page says it all with a display of brilliant colors in vertical stripes.

If there's enough time before your wedding anniversary (or that special someone's birthday, or Mother's Day) you might be able to whip up a cake-card several tiers high and decorate it with candles. What better way to say "congratulations!" The hole puncher helps to create the small dots.

Sometimes "just a sliver" of cake will be appreciated just as much! Just remember to add the whipped cream!

Those who don't care about sweets might be much happier receiving a floral bouquet. The front page is lavishly decorated. In the lower right corner there's a single blossom (with two leaves cut out) on all but the last two pages. For a colorful effect, glue colored paper to the back page.

Festive cocktails, colorful garnish—an evening right out of the Arabian Nights! These invitations beg you to join the fun. Why not send one of these cards for no particular reason? The silhouette of a Moorish palace is a clever decorating device that a grateful recipient might be able to use for his own special occasion.

The row of colorful cocktails on the le[ft] becomes a full bar when the card is fu[lly] opened. This card could also decorate yo[ur] bar at home. Who wouldn't accept an in[vi]tation if it looked like this?

The champagne glass opens from [the] bottom up, and the dots—imitating bu[b]bles rising to the top—are made using a ho[le] puncher.

The crescent moon and the stars are all
cutouts that carry through to every page.
Wonderful effects can be achieved by
gluing different-colored paper on the back
of each page.

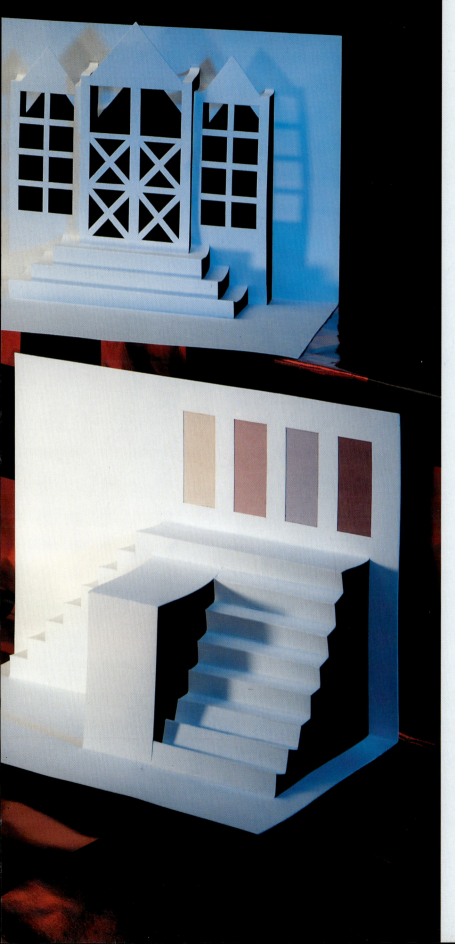

PAPER ARCHITEC-TURE

Compared to the two-dimensional collage cards, or to the folding cards with somewhat limited spatial effects, the examples of the three-dimensional forms found here (reminiscent of true architectural designs) will astound you. These three-dimensional pop-up creations never fail to surprise. What makes them so fascinating?

These hollow sculptures are created by simply following a certain basic cutting-and-folding method, and they never require a single drop of glue. When these cards are closed they stay flat. When they're opened, they unfold into three-dimensional structures.

Where did the idea for turning a flat piece of paper into a three-dimensional structure come from? You might have guessed—from Asia! With the well-known art of paper-folding (origami), paper architecture is an important Asian tradition for the creative use of paper.

Inspired by this centuries-old Japanese technique, artists at the Bauhaus school in Germany, earlier in this century, recognized that paper was a useful medium in its own right. Almost ignored until then, paper began to play an important role at the Bauhaus, where concepts of new architectural forms were unfolding. The Bauhaus artists examined and tested the material, free from preconceived, academic notions, and attempted to use paper appropriately.

One result of this work was the inspiration for the greeting cards in this chapter.

Technique

The easiest and fastest way to become familiar with the concept underlying pop-up cards is to duplicate one of the examples in this book. Before going into detailed instructions, let's say a few words about the pattern.

Naturally, these cards can be made in many different sizes: small enough to tuck into an envelope or big enough to use as room decorations. Depending upon your dexterity, the strength of the paper plays a very important role. The patterns for these pop-up cards can be found at the back of this book.

If the patterns are too small for your purposes, enlarge them to the desired size using a photocopier at 121%. This should enlarge the patterns at 83% to full size. Most modern copiers can enlarge. Position the appropriate page of the book face down on the copier's glass surface and choose an enlargment (usually 121%) to suit your needs. Personnel in the copy shop will help you. Should that size still not satisfy you, enlarge parts of the design separately and join them afterwards. Make sure that you use strong cardboard for an oversize project.

After you've chosen a design, make a copy of the (enlarged) pattern on tracing paper, using a soft pencil and a ruler. Tape the tracing paper on top of the pattern.

Now choose either white cardboard or light-colored construction paper and cut the paper to its proper size. Be generous when measuring the size of the card to prevent part of the design from extending beyond the edges when the card is finished. It's easy enough to cut down the card to the desired size after everything is finished.

One method for transferring a pattern to the face of a card was described in the chapter on folding cards (see page 24). Here's a second method. Using the same materials you used for the first method, copy the lines of the pattern onto the trac-

Illus. 17

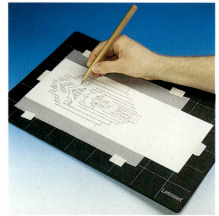

Illus. 18

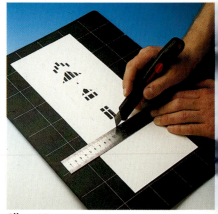

Illus. 19

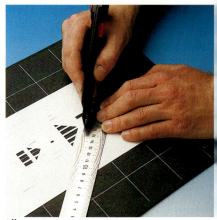

Illus. 20

ing paper (see Illus. 17). Secure the tracing paper with tape, as you did before. Detach the tape and turn the tracing paper over, and place it on the face of the card. Now, redraw the lines you originally traced. This should transfer the soft lead lines to the front of the card.

It's important to remember that there are two kinds of line. Make sure you check the patterns as they're shown in this book. Dashed lines are those that will be creased using only the tip of the utility knife (folding can then be accomplished cleanly and easily). Solid lines (on the other hand) will actually be cut.

For a pop-up card to function properly, follow instructions very carefully: Exact pattern transfer, precise cutting and creasing are the most important steps. If you're patient and very careful, and follow the sequence of the individual steps, the rest will be easy.

Here's yet a third method for transferring simple, straight lines. The advantage of this method is that you don't have to remove pencil marks. The disadvantage is

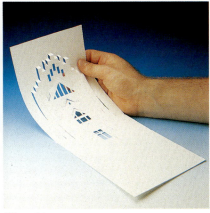

Illus. 21

Illus. 22

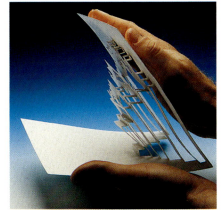

Illus. 23

that you must be even more careful when you check the pattern. Place the copy of the design pattern on the cardboard and protect the tabletop underneath it with a sturdy pad.

Prevent the top sheet from moving (tape it down) and then punch small holes through the pattern paper (using a pin or a needle), on every corner of the design and at all points where lines cross each other (see Illus. 18). You can connect these points/holes with either dashed lines or solid pencil lines, following the design pattern. If you've already developed some expertise, skip this last step (pencilling the lines) and proceed to the next step, checking the pattern and the instructions at all times.

Whenever the design has been transferred (no matter which method of transfer you've chosen), crease the cardboard along the dashed lines and cut along the solid lines. Don't be hasty—that leads to mix-ups. Don't extend or shorten the crease lines, nor the cutting lines. Use your metal ruler as a guide for cutting or creasing the straight lines—it makes your work easier and your finished project will look all the more impressive (see Illus. 19).

When you cut those lines of the design that end in a corner or a tip, move the tip

of the cutter *towards* the corner or the tip, not *away* from it; you'll avoid bending or tearing the paper there (see Illus. 20).

When you're finished, check every solid line and every dashed line to make sure that you didn't miss any, because each individual line is important with this intricate folding system. If you missed cutting one line, or you cut one line that was not intended to be cut, you might not be able to properly fold the card together. Generally, mistakes made either in transferring or cutting can't be corrected. Now you can erase pencil marks, but only after you've completed this last important "quality control."

Now comes the exciting part of the process, and it will be the final test to see if you've carefully followed all of the instructions. Start (carefully) to push out every part of the design from the back. Start from the top and work down. The card should be folded forward on the uppermost folding line and backwards (down) on the folding line that's immediately beneath it. Continue in this way until you reach the end (see Illus. 21). The horizontal line that folds the card in half also should be folded forward. You will notice that all this is rather simple, because you can see the design developing by itself as you fold and unfold.

After this initial folding, during which all the different parts of the design are pulled out, carefully reinforce every fold, because by now you should have a good idea of how your creation should look. If you encounter a problem, flatten the card and check back with the pattern. You may be able to correct small errors. Pull out the smaller portions of the design using a pair of tweezers (see Illus. 22).

If you've worked with the necessary exactness, it will be easy to fold down the three-dimensional paper project (see Illus. 23). Lift the top of the card to display the design impressively.

Illus. 24

Experiment with Color

Illus. 25

Light and shadow and light dark contrasts are critical factors in the spatial effect of these folded paper objects. Two identical designs will look different if they're illuminated differently.

Most of the examples we've chosen here are made using white sketch-pad paper, or only very lightly colored construction paper. The lighter the paper's color, the more striking the light/shadow contrast and the more impressive the graphic effect.

When the card is backlit, the effect is stunning. This backlighting makes many of the designs perfect window displays. Those designs whose detailed structures are arranged one behind the other look very much like stage props, due to the illusion of depth.

You could glue contrasting-color paper to the back of a card. This backing adds stability to those designs with large or very intricate patterns, and it also adds unexpected color. Imagine receiving a greeting card that (on first glance) appears rather plain, only to find a piece of wonderful and intricate paper architecture inside! Whenever a vivid background is illuminated against the white of the design, new, soft nuances are created.

Measure the contrasting-color paper that you'll be using for the background to precisely fit the back of your greeting card, or allow the colored paper to extend slightly beyond the edges, to act as a frame. When the card is closed, nothing of the inside structure should extend beyond the edge of the card. Crease the midline slightly, using the utility knife.

Be sure that the contrasting paper is glued *only* to the uncut portion of the card, and not to those parts that will unfold. Glue the two lower halves together first, and then lift the top half at a right angle before gluing the two upper portions (see Illus. 24). This step makes it easier to open and close the card after the glue has dried. Gluing a card and its background together while they're both opened flat on the table can create problems.

Additional accents can easily be added by gluing construction paper (in contrasting colors) behind the cutouts. You might consider using gift-wrap paper with a pretty print. Well-planned projects, of course, make it possible to glue such paper to the front page of the card before starting to cut out the design (see Illus. 25). To be sure that your project remains flexible, fold the paper that's directly above the folding line of the card at a 90° angle before gluing it into place.

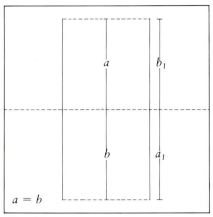

Illus. 26

Tips for Your Own Creations

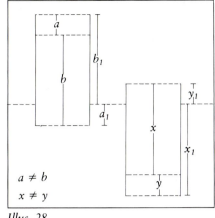

Illus. 28

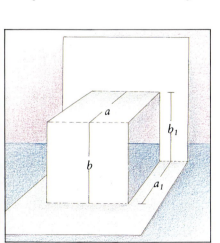

Illus. 27

After trying some of the examples in this book, you might be tempted to try your own ideas for a pop-up card. If that's the case, let's briefly go over the basic characteristics of paper architecture.

The shape of the structure is controlled by 90° angles. The card's surfaces are either parallel to each other or at right angles to each other. Only vertical and horizontal planes exist. The line that separates the two halves of the card is in the middle—it's called the "main folding line." It's from this line that all the design's subsequent creasing lines and cutting lines are made.

Depending upon the position of the pattern in relation to the main folding line, we talk about either symmetrical or asymmetrical folds.

The easiest of the two folds is the symmetrical fold, since all parts of the design are equidistant from the main folding line

(see Illus. 26 and Illus. 27). Horizontal surface "a" is identical in length to vertical surface "b". Both dash lines (on the top and on the bottom) are also equidistant from the vertical midline and the main folding line.

Illus. 28 and Illus. 29 show two examples of asymmetrical folds. Here the vertical distance differs from the horizontal distance ($a \neq b$ and $x \neq y$). You could choose any height or width for a form; that doesn't mean, however, that you can draw lines at random! It's very important that the distance of all three folding lines of a design be in proper relation to each other as well as to the main folding line. A parallel displacement of the pop-up portion of the card occurs when you open it, so be sure that $a = a_1$, $b = b_1$, $x = x_1$, and $y = y_1$. Illus. 28 clearly explains this principle. A card whose dimensions aren't measured correctly, or are out of proportion, will have surfaces that aren't straight, and the card won't close properly.

When you have patterns where additional portions pop out of already existing

ones (as is the case with many of the patterns), proceed in the same way. Use the lower folding line of the preceding pop-out as the main folding line on which to align the other three lines of the new pop-out. Use this method when you want to create staircases. If, in addition, you add cutouts and elements that won't pop up automatically when the card is unfolded (a fence, group of bushes, etc.), you'll create some wonderful paper objects. You could even use round shapes in your pop-up creations. Your design shouldn't be *too* complicated. It should express simplicity with the use of geometrical forms.

Before you begin your project, whether you're making greeting cards, place cards, notes, menus, window displays, or room decorations, test your own design first, using typing paper.

Now have fun with paper architecture!

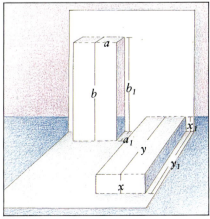

Illus. 29

Architectural themes are ideal for pop-up cards. A staircase makes a particularly striking design.

The staircase on the left is not difficult to make. Steps that narrow gradually towards the top, while keeping a uniform height, give an even, flowing rhythm to the design. The vertical cutouts, highlighted with a muted print (gift-wrap paper) serve as a perfect accent. A strong print might detract from the overall design. It's not hard to create your own contrasting paper; you could use watercolor or crayons.

The example on the bottom of the facing page is mainly symmetrical, although an asymmetrical folding method (pages 38–39) is necessary for this design.

Egg-shaped forms, arranged one in front of the other, create a very three-dimensional structure. The abstract shape, however, could also represent other organic forms—a tree, perhaps, or a tulip. This example shows well that it's not necessary to work exclusively with straight lines.

Another example, using a staircase design, is shown immediately to the left, with steps ranged on both sides. Vertical strips of different lengths are made from construction paper, and they're glued to the surface of the card. They balance and offset the staircase design.

41

All types of vehicle can be constructed with the pop-up technique, if their forms are reduced to their essential lines. From the point of view of design and cutting technique, most of the elements used to build them are straight lines.

Who wouldn't accept an invitation to go on a luxurious cruise when the invitation comes with this dream boat? This card would also be a very unusual greeting card sent from a cruise or from an exotic port.

Here's a perfect card for the passionate sailor. Little flags made from construction paper serve as colorful accents. The blue stripes glued to the white paper are simplified ocean waves.

The paper car will delight not only those who are passionate about classic cars. This could be a "congratulations" card for one who's just received his first driver's license.

The nostalgic locomotive with its tender and one car might take a bit of time to make. It will be a sure hit with true railroad buffs.

42

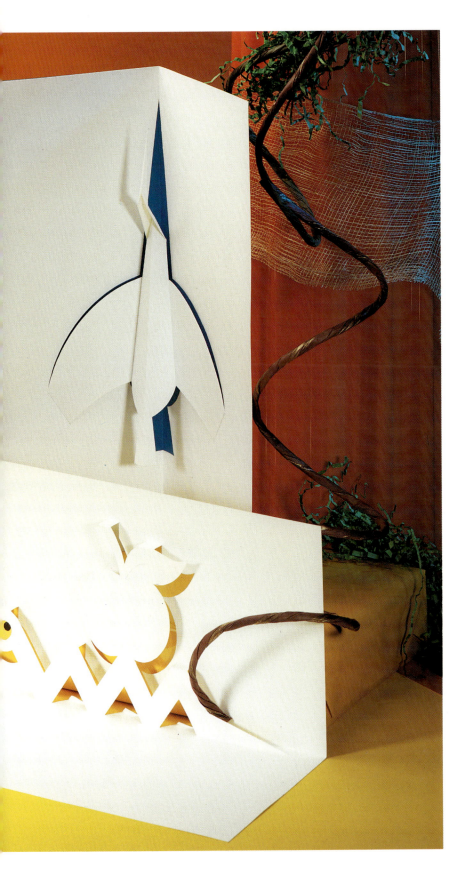

The examples shown on these two pages are not very difficult to make.

The beetle is a typical example of the symmetrical folding technique. Each cut and crease is equidistant from the main folding line of the card. The beetle is a relatively realistic representation of the real thing, while the crane (a card for beginners) is an essentially abstract design.

All the other cards are made with the asymmetrical folding technique, although the elephant and the goat themselves are symmetrical (see the drawings and the instructions on pages 38–39). If you need a birthday card for a Capricorn, you're in luck—here's a design ready to be copied! Expand on this theme and create your own cards for other signs of the zodiac.

The elephant, the goat, and the seductive snake all have little accents made from construction paper. These cards would be wonderful to use as place cards for a dinner party. Children *and* adults will fall in love with them.

The two houses on the facing page are examples of how well suited "architectural" designs are for the pop-up technique. Both real houses and cards made with this technique use an arrangement of true 90° angles, straight lines, and parallel lines.

These miniature stage settings—this kind of paper art—bring pleasure all year.

The country house on the far right is surrounded by lush greenery. The contrast between the straight lines and the rounded forms makes this design particularly charming. The spatial arrangement adds its own effect.

The house in the middle has a fence that's independent of the pop-up design. The fence is pulled out of the background separately—it won't come up automatically. The fence height isn't a mistake. I

wanted to add depth to the scene by making the fence disproportionately large.

The bushes surrounding the reindeer must be pulled up separately after the card has been opened. Only the two bushes on either side of the reindeer are part of the pop-up. The eyes are made of construction paper that's been glued behind the eye holes.

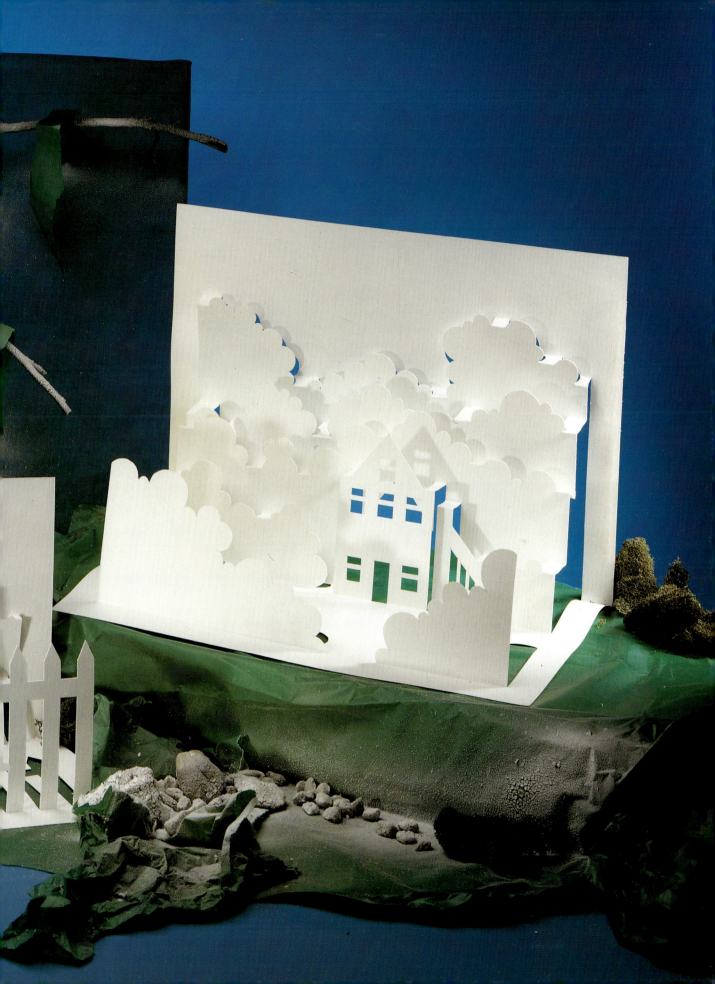

The theme is love and marriage. These cards tell the whole story, from the first "butterflies in the tummy" to the wedding cake.

Of course, these cards could be used for other occasions. A cake is also a must for birthdays or anniversaries. Although no fattening treats are promised, the card itself is "appetizing." This card will still be kept long after the festivities are over.

And below, spelled out in great big letters—L O V E.

The butterfly, made using the symmetrical folding technique on pages 38–39, is cut out of the white paper before the decorative accents (made from construction paper) are glued to the back. You can choose your own color combinations or you could use delicate gift-wrap paper.

The church would also make a wonderful Christmas card. Long, vertical columns are the main elements of this simple abstract design.

White and delicately colored papers are suitable for pop-up projects. Contrasted with dark backgrounds, the effects of light/shadow bring out the depth and the spatial aspects of the designs.

The house on the far left, with its richly constructed facade, has other interesting elements—stairlike and pointed gable roofs. Foreground surfaces (pulled up separately when the card is opened) add depth to the design.

The New Year's card in the middle spells out the year as an integral part of its design. This "year" motif could be used for other occasions: the anniversary of a company's founding, a wedding anniversary, or a birthday. Names or special greetings could be committed to paper by using this technique.

"Onward and upward!" Optimism can be contagious when you send this card. This example of paper architecture, with its great depth, could help express "Best wishes for a speedy recovery" or "Congratulations on your promotion." To add an interesting accent, the cutout was highlighted by gluing marbleized paper behind it.

Although a wide variety of greeting cards and notepaper sets is available, envelopes (in general) are available only in white or in pastel colors.

ENVELOPES

Reach for a pair of scissors, glue and paper, and create your own envelopes. Now you can match an envelope in size and style to the individual card you want to create, and not the other way around.

Take an ordinary envelope in a shade you like and give it a new face by dressing it up with pretty paper. A few contrasting accents in the form of circles, squares, or triangles are usually all that's necessary to turn a plain envelope into a work of art.

Don't be satisfied with just a "remodelling" job—design your own envelopes and make them fit the greeting cards you've already made. You'll find suggestions in this chapter for envelopes in different shapes.

The envelope's size depends on the card's size. To determine the envelope's correct size, add some space to the card's outer dimensions. The card can be inserted easily then. The envelope's shape always follows the card's shape. The individual parts of the envelope overlap when the envelope is closed.

First test your envelope design using newspaper. Transfer the envelope's design to the paper of your choice (construction paper works well) and carefully crease all the dashed lines, using a utility knife to ensure clean folds. Fold the side flaps to the center, put a little glue on the top edge of the lower flap and fold it up to the middle, gluing it to the edges of the side flaps. When closing the envelope, use only a little drop of glue, or better yet, tuck the flap inside the envelope.

This saves the envelope (or its contents) from damage when it's opened.

There are at least as many possibilities for designing your own envelopes as there are for designing greeting cards. I picked only a few to give you an idea of what can be done. Since the size of the envelope depends upon the size of the card that goes into it, we haven't given you any specific patterns. Anyway, it's easy enough to copy the examples given here. The examples might serve as an inspiration for your own creativity.

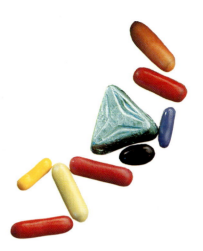

The envelopes on the far left clearly demonstrate how easy it is to give a new face to an envelope using just a few border accents. Choose between horizontal or vertical stripes, in one or many different colors, wide or narrow, and so on. For the envelopes on the near left, however, the placement of the address was taken into account, and the available space was divided accordingly. Two envelopes show bold zigzag designs, while the two others show what can be done with curved designs.

The envelopes in the lower-left corner present the dramatic effects of diagonal elements. The diagonal separation runs from one corner to the other on some envelopes. On others, the diagonal line is shifted more to the left to highlight one of the corners. You could combine several diagonal lines, or you could create contrast between round shapes and straight lines, as seen on one of the envelopes in the upper left-hand corner.

You could design an envelope and divide its surface in half, horizontally, vertically, or even off-center. Stripes add accent and optical emphasis to the envelopes. The envelope at near-left is like a gift sent "air-mail." The design is similar to the red, white, and black envelope next to it. The red-black contrast gives this card a certain grand elegance.

The cloudlike shape with the black stripes (bottom middle) is an envelope design that's independent of the shape of the card. The card has to be small enough to fit inside.

PATTERNS

Tips on using the patterns: Dashed lines are always creased, never cut. If a pattern has many repeated forms (small circles, dots, triangles, or stripes), only a few have been included on the pattern. Finish your card according to the photos shown.

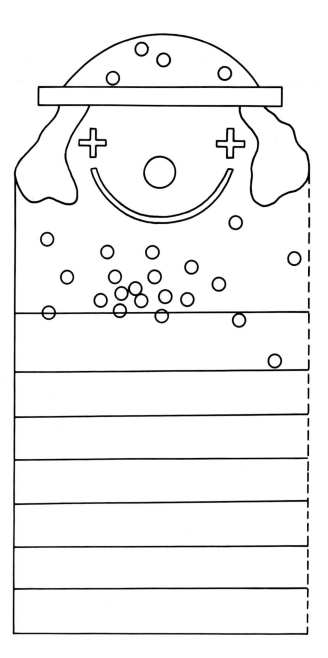

Page 1
83%

Title Page 83%

Page 10
83%

Page 11
83%

Page 14   83%

Page 14
83%

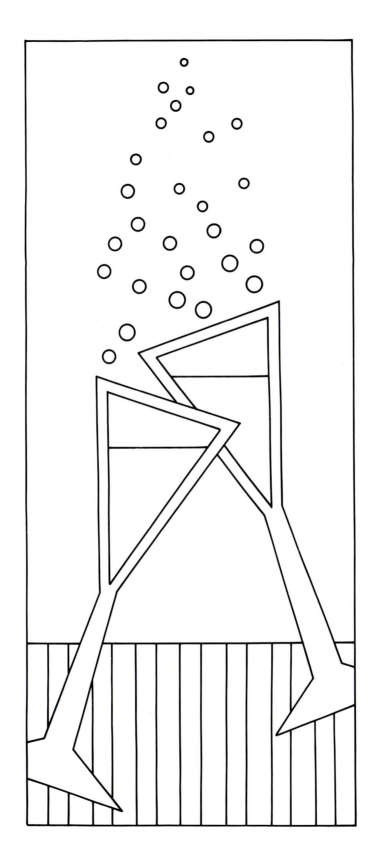

Page 15
83%

Page 15
83%

Pages 14–15
83%

Page 16
83%

Page 16
83%

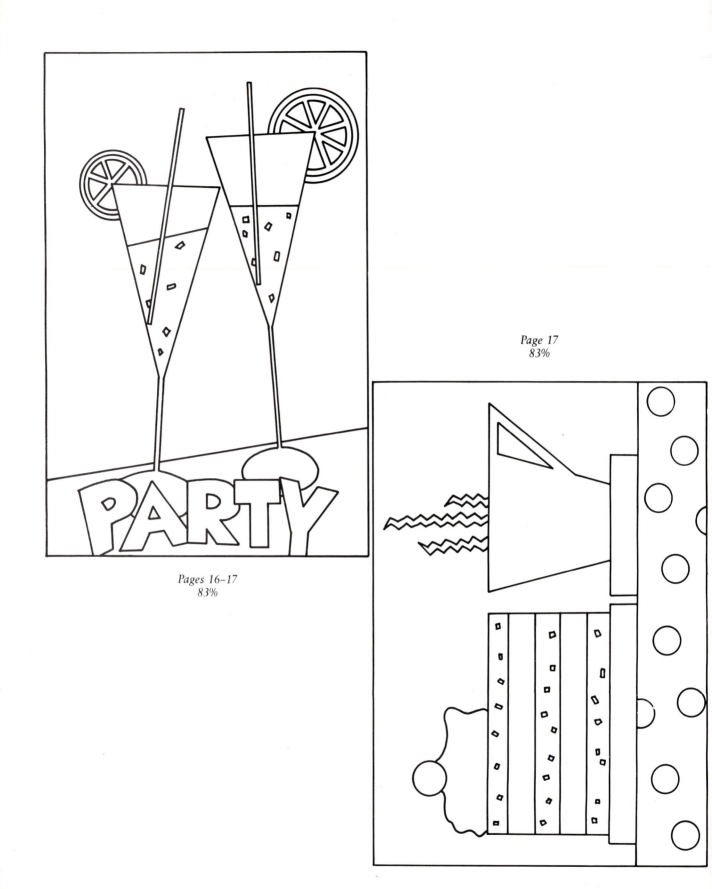

Pages 16–17
83%

Page 17
83%

Page 17
83%

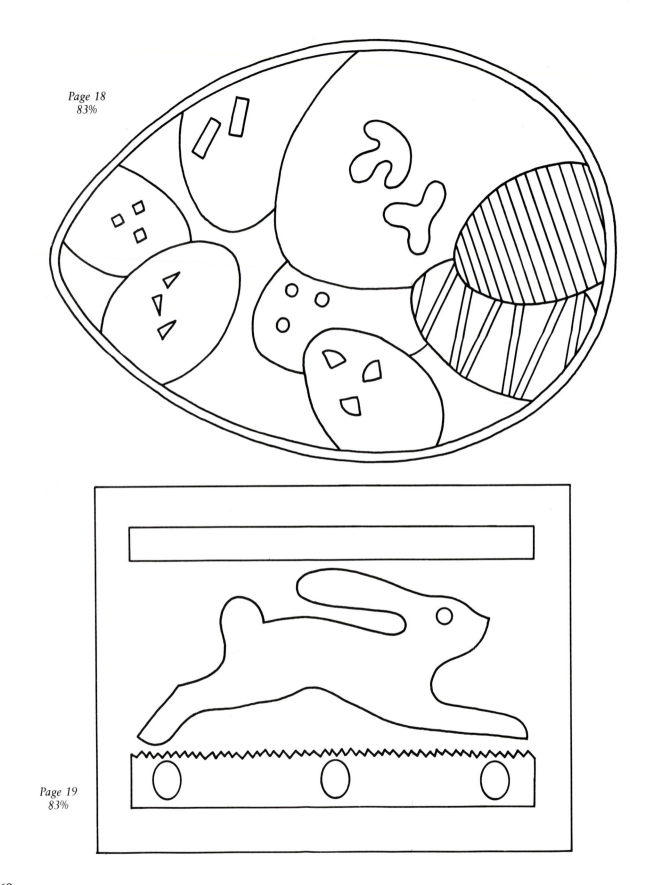

Page 18
83%

Page 19
83%

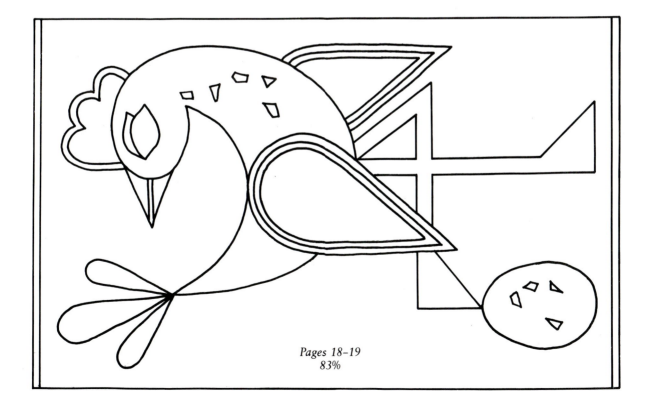

Pages 18–19
83%

Page 19
83%

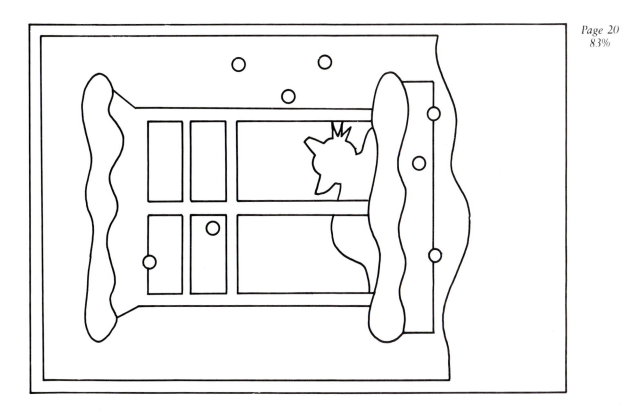

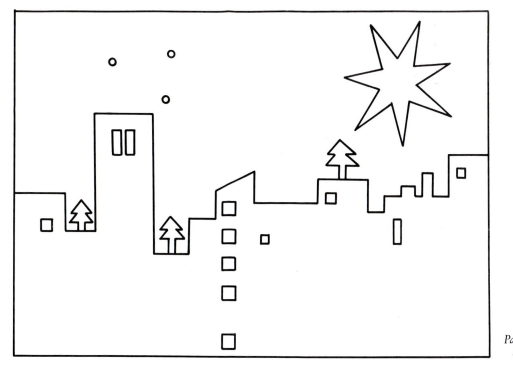

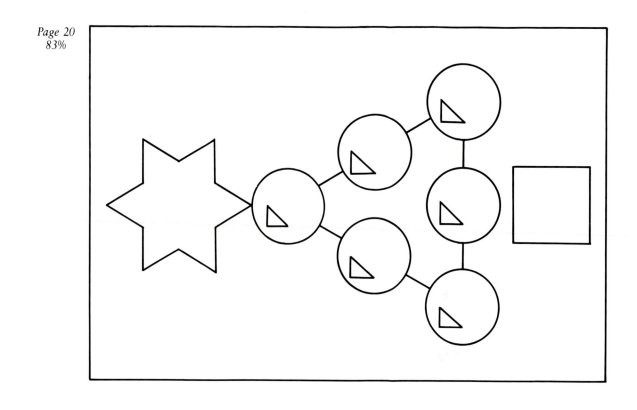

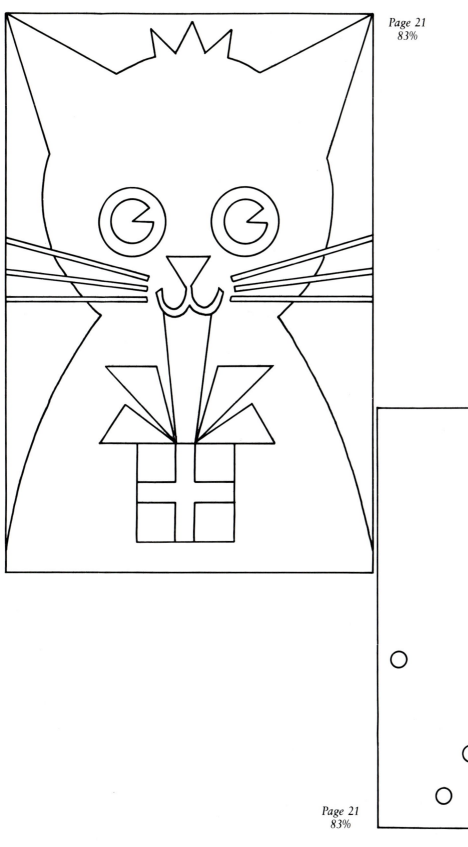

Page 22
83%

Pages 22
83%

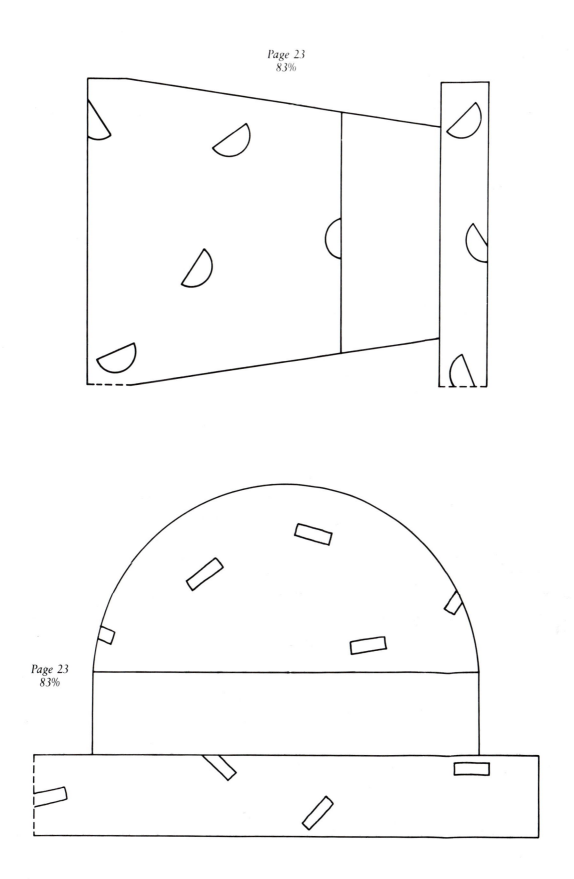

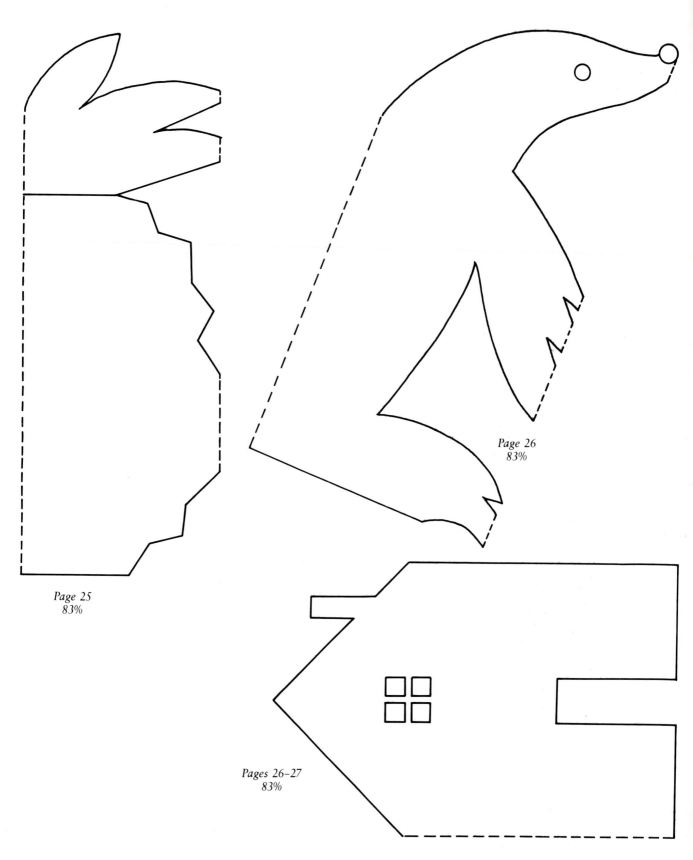

Page 25
83%

Page 26
83%

Pages 26–27
83%

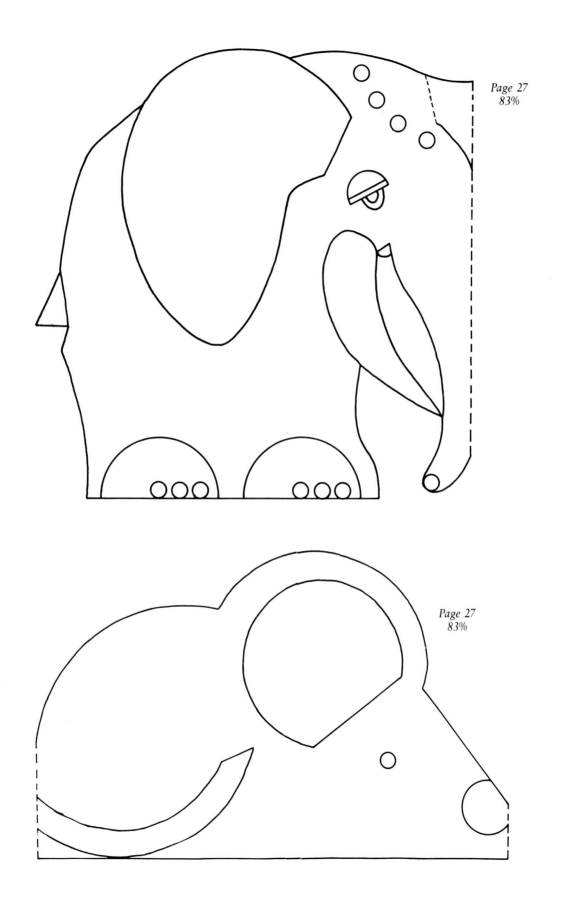

Page 27
83%

Page 27
83%

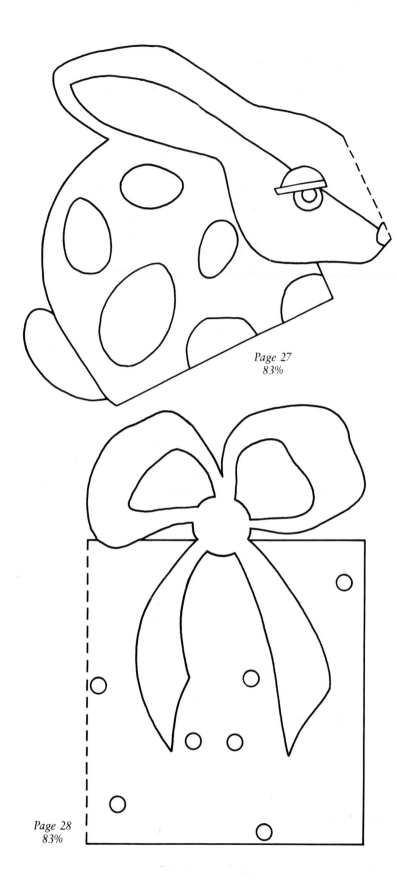

Page 27
83%

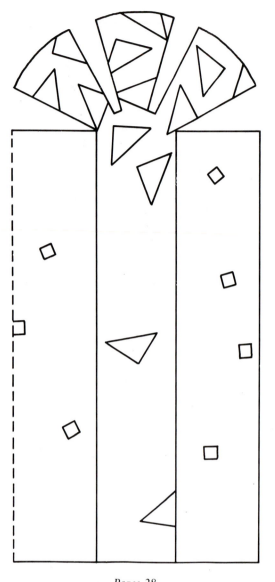

Pages 28
83%

Page 28
83%

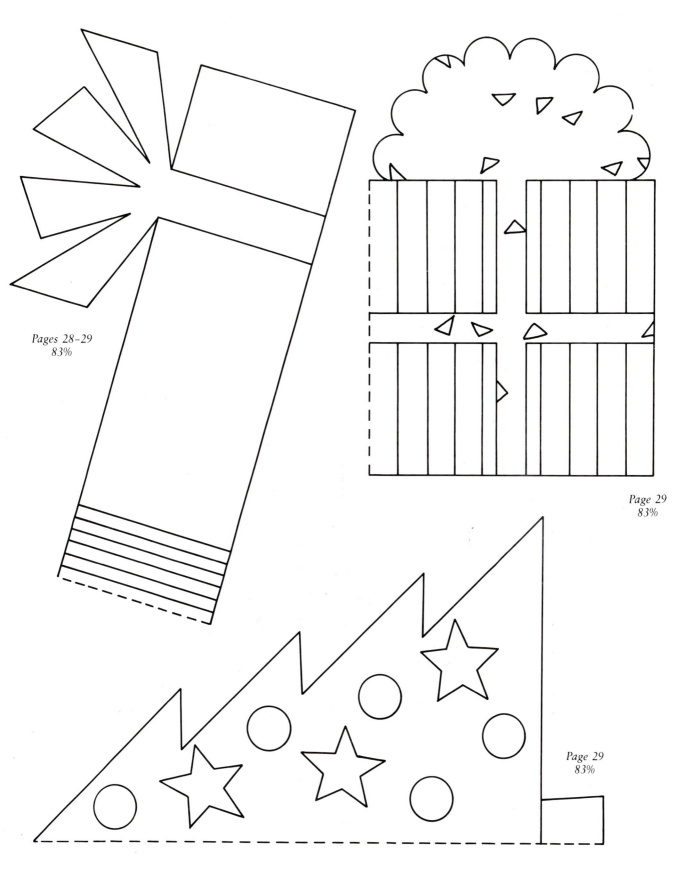

Pages 28–29
83%

Page 29
83%

Page 29
83%

Page 30
83%

Page 30
83%

80

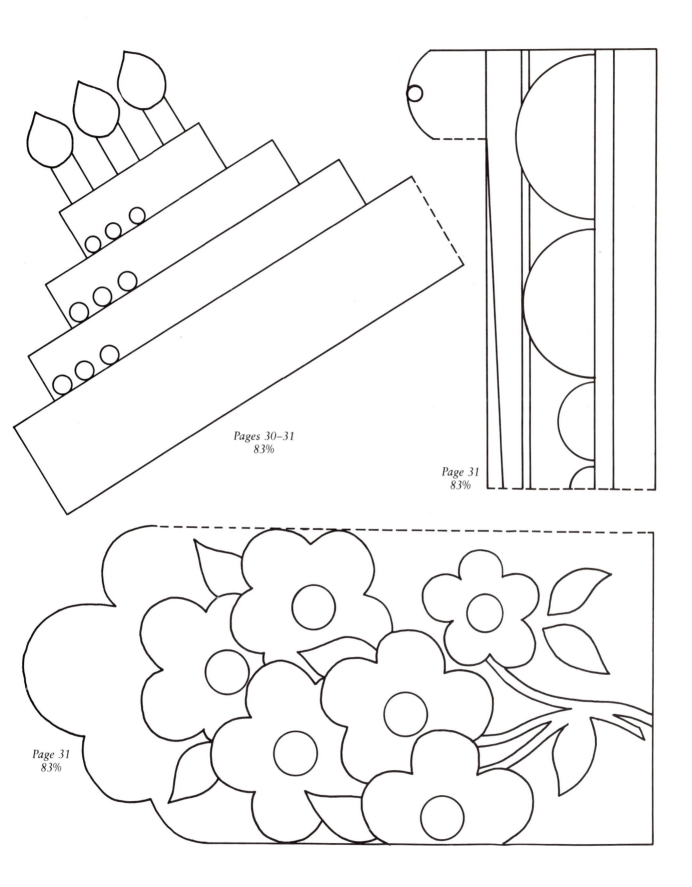

Pages 30–31
83%

Page 31
83%

Page 31
83%

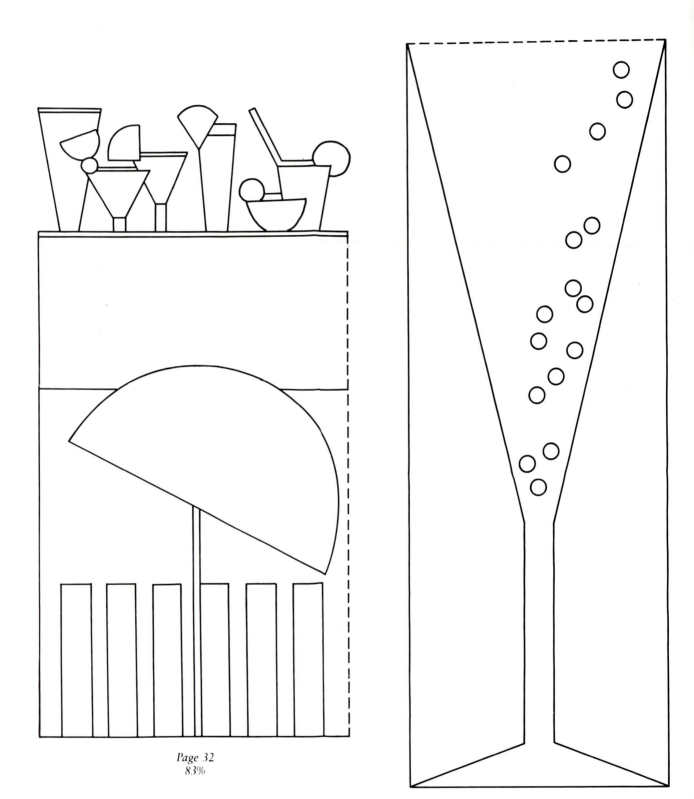

Page 32
83%

Page 33
83%

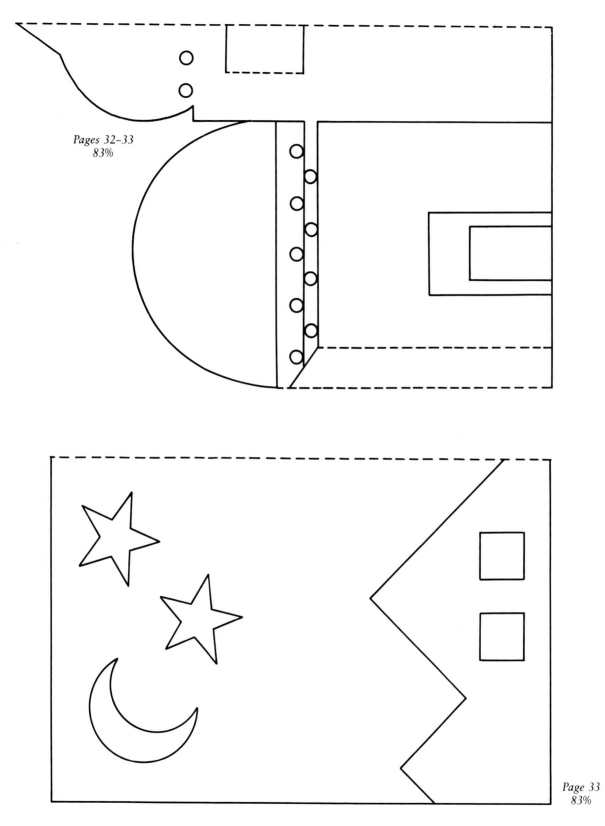

Pages 32–33
83%

Page 33
83%

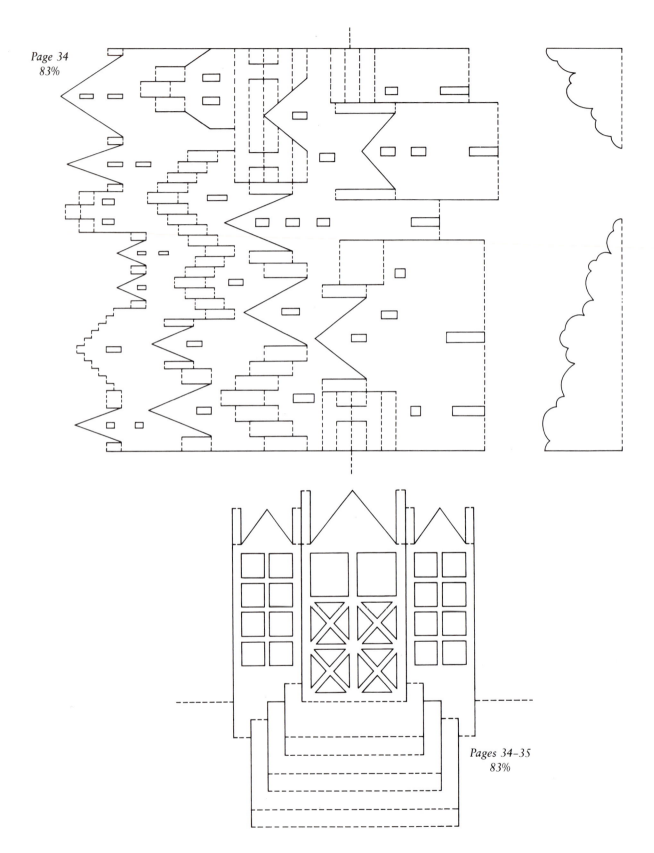

Page 34
83%

Pages 34–35
83%

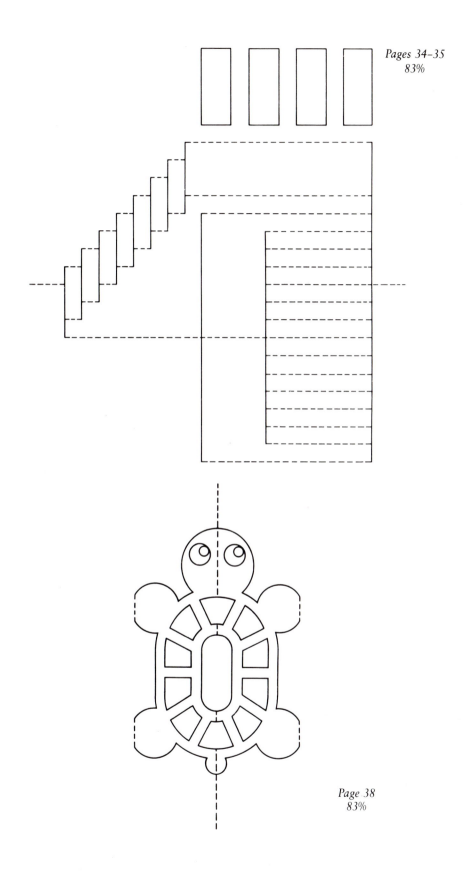

Pages 34–35
83%

Page 38
83%

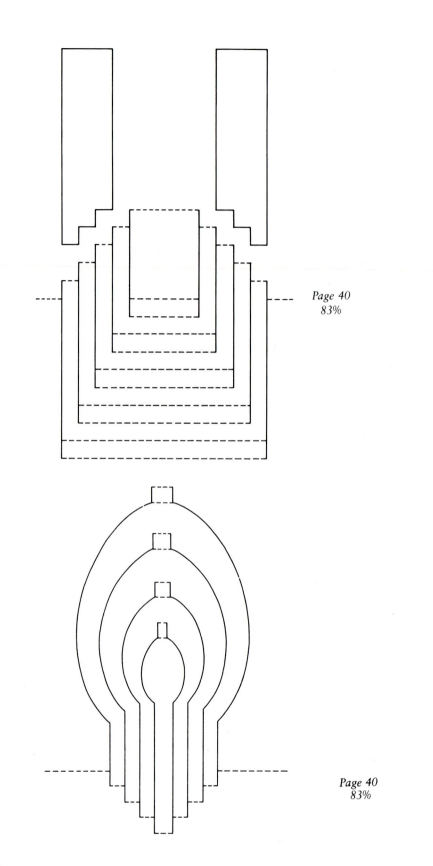

Page 40
83%

Page 40
83%

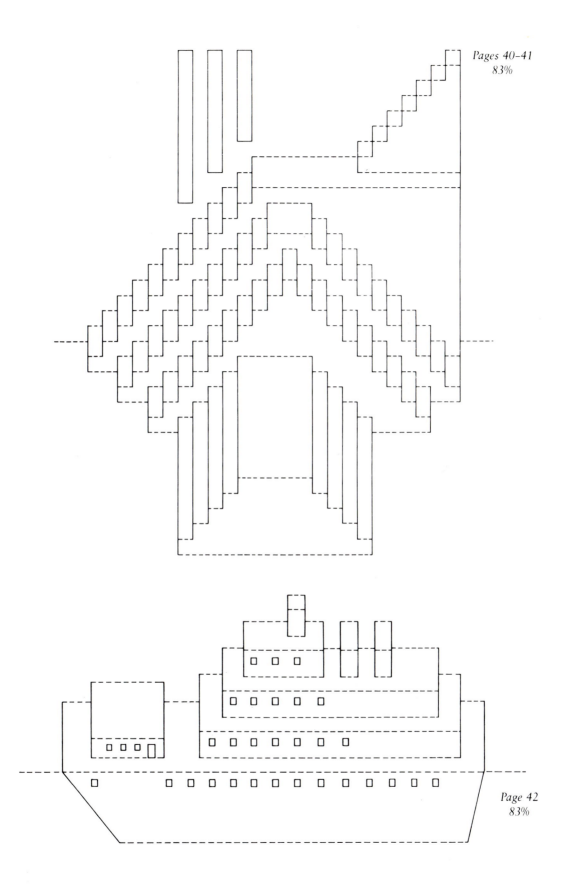

Pages 40–41
83%

Page 42
83%

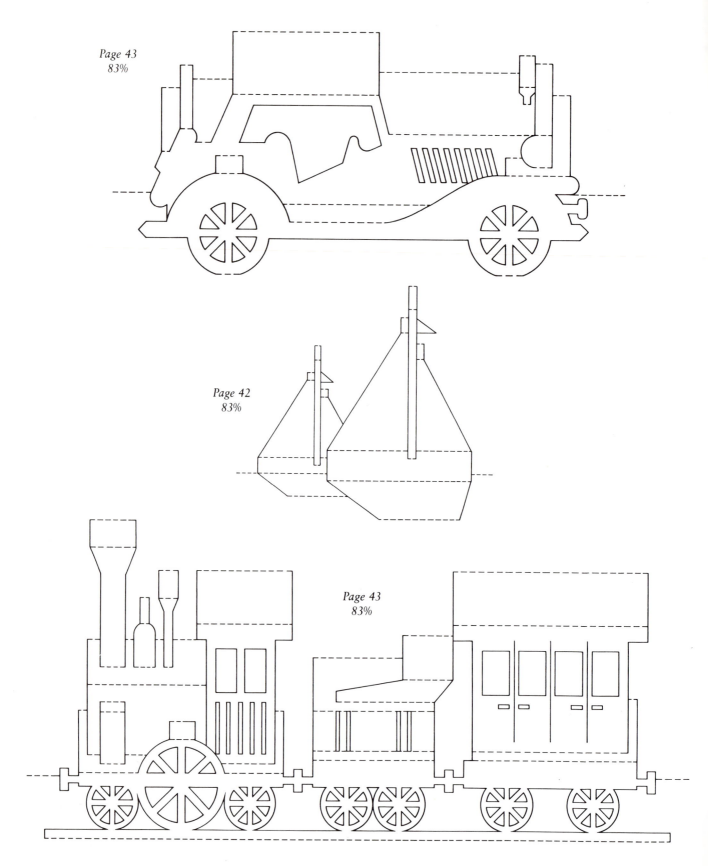

Page 43
83%

Page 42
83%

Page 43
83%

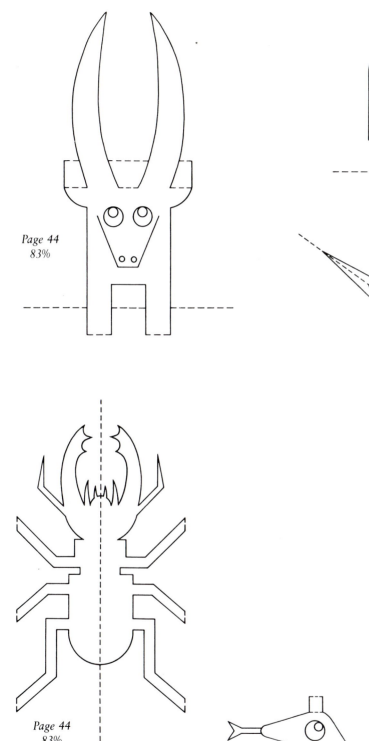

Page 44
83%

Page 44
83%

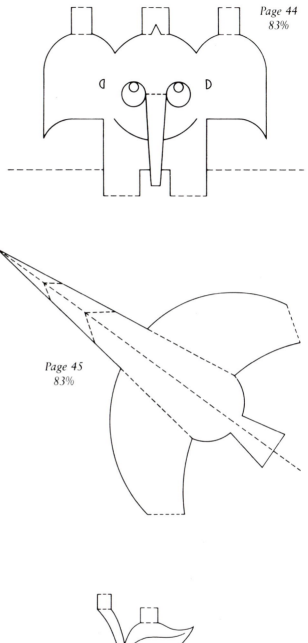

Page 44
83%

Page 45
83%

Page 45
83%

Pages 46–47
83%

Page 46
83%

90

Page 47
83%

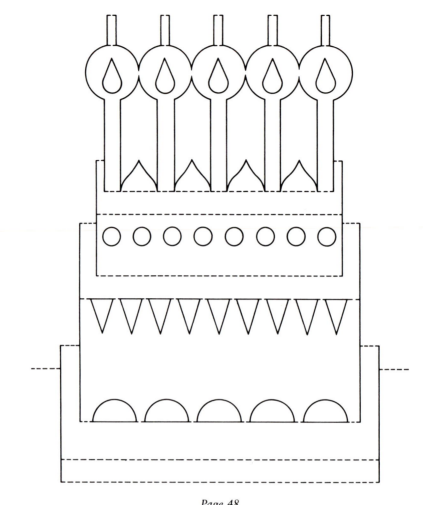

Page 48
83%

Page 49
83%

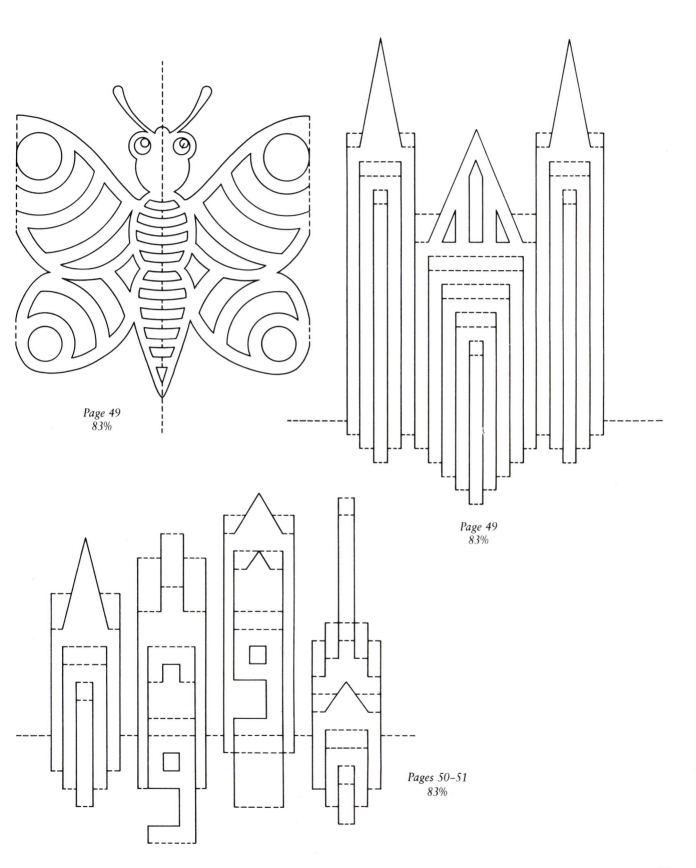

Page 49
83%

Page 49
83%

Pages 50–51
83%

93

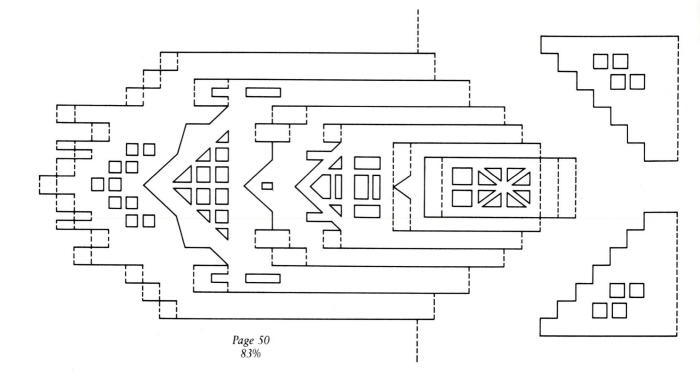

Page 50
83%

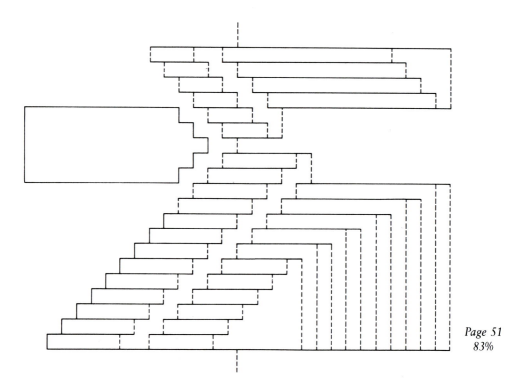

Page 51
83%

94

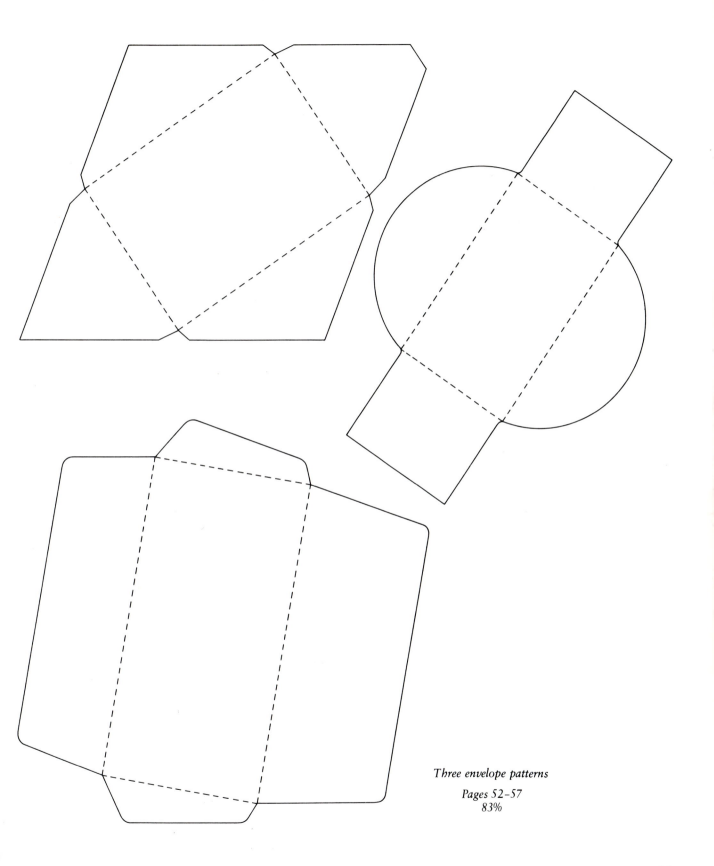

Three envelope patterns
Pages 52–57
83%

95

Special thanks to the following graphic designers:

Petra Beutl Page 25 (Pineapple), Pages 26–27 (Elephant, Sea Lion, Mouse, Rabbit), Page 31 (Slice of Cake), Pages 32–33 (Moroccan Palace)

Matthias Bumiller Page 21 (Mushroom)

Sabine Dichtler Pages 28–29 (Red Package, Christmas Tree), Pages 30–31 (Cake with Candles, Thanks, Sorry, Floral Bouquet, Pages 32–33 (Moonlit Night, Cocktails)

Burkhard Finken Page 19 (Bounding Rabbit), Pages 26–27 (Row Houses)

Anna Kraft Page 17 (Coffee and Cake, Party Invitation), Page 20 (Cityscape)

The remaining examples are by the author.

Commercial use of any of these designs is prohibited.

Photos: Michael Zorn

Drawings: Grafik Design Horn (pages 12–13, 38, 39)

Pattern Drawings: Ulrike Hoffmann

Graphic Design: Silvia Pohlmann

Suggestions given in this book have been carefully checked by the author as well as by the publishers, but no guarantees are given. The author, the publishers, and their representatives are not liable for damages to persons or property, nor for monetary losses.

INDEX

Antique Train 43
Ascending Hearts 14
Baby in an Egg 22
Beach 16
Beetle 44
Big City 34
Birthday Cake 48
Blossoms 19
Blue Hat 23
Blue Package 28
Bounding Rabbit 19
Butterfly 49
Cake with Candles 30–31
Cat in a Window 20
Cat with a Gift 21
Champagne Bubbles 33
Champagne Glasses 5, 15
Christmas Tree 20
Church 49
Ciao 16
Circus Elephant 27
Cityscape 20
Classic Car 43
Clown 1
Cocktails 32
Coffee and Cake 17
Collage Cards 11
Crane 45
Easter Egg 18
Elephant 44
Envelopes 52–57
Experiment with Color 38
Fender Bender 14–15
Floral Bouquet 31
Folded Christmas Tree 29
Folding Cards 23
Goat 44
Grand Staircase 35
Hallo 22
Hard Rock 4, 10
Hen 19
History of Paper 6

Keyboard 14
Lilies 19
Love 48–49
Love Hearts 15
Lovers 2–3
Lucky Pig 21
Luxury Liner 42
Marble Stairway 51
Mardi Gras 17
Materials and Supplies 8–9
Maze 41
Moonlit Night 33
Moroccan Palace 4, 32–33
Mouse 27
Mushroom 21
Oscar Night 40
Paper Architecture 35–51
Paper Manufacturing 6
Party Invitation 16–17
Patterns 58–95
Picket Fence 46–47
Pineapple 25
Pink and Purple Package 29
Rabbit 4, 27
Red Package 28
Reindeer 46
Row Houses 26
Sailboat 42
Sea Lion 26
Skyscraper 50
Slice of Cake 31
Snake 45
Sorry 30
Stage Set 35
Technique 12, 24, 36
Thanks 30
Tropical Blossoms 11
Tulip 40
Uses for Paper 7
Year 50–51
Yellow and Purple Package 28–29
Woodland Cottage 47